LIVERPOOL
The Great City

PAUL MCMULLIN
TEXT BY MIKE MCNAMEE

HALSGROVE

First published in Great Britain in 2015
Reprinted 2017
Copyright © Paul McMullin and Mike McNamee 2015

British Library Cataloguing-in-Publication Data
A CIP record for this title is available from the British Library

ISBN 978 0 85704 272 9

HALSGROVE

Halsgrove House, Ryelands Business Park,
Bagley Road, Wellington, Somerset TA21 9PZ
Tel: 01823 653777   Fax: 01823 216796
email: sales@halsgrove.com

Part of the Halsgrove group of companies
Information on all Halsgrove titles is
available at: www.halsgrove.com

Printed in India by Parksons Graphics

FOREWORD
by Tom Dykes

This is home; I love this city. Liverpool has played a major role in the economic and cultural life not just of the United Kingdom but also of the USA, Canada and many other nations. As an ex-pat who, in 1965 aged 24, left the Pier Head on board Cunard's *Carinthia* bound for Montreal, I had no idea that I would spend the next 50 years as a promoter and booster of all things Liverpool.

Over the half century since the leaving of Liverpool, I evolved as a 'carrier of messages and the teller of truths' about my city. Distance made my Liverpool DNA even more pronounced and my experiences growing up through the war and post war periods galvanized my Liverpool pride. Seeing the phoenix-like emergence of spirit from the devastation of the Blitz imprinted itself upon me.

Thousands of Canadian high school students from British Columbia to Ontario gained 'added value' to their educational experiences as they became aware of the role my city played in the development of Canada. From an active role in the establishment of Canadian Confederation through Liverpool-born John Mercer Johnson to the key role in the Battle of the Atlantic, young Canadians acquired an SQ or Scouse Quotient.

As an education consultant with American police services, I was also able to bring the message of Liverpool's role in the evolution of the USA! I was almost evangelical in my zeal to inform the Boys in Blue from Baton Rouge to Boston that it was Robert Morris, a scouser, who financed their revolution; that Harvard had its roots in the Mathers of Toxteth and that the final signing of surrender by the Confederacy was in Liverpool!

Pride in my city and my heritage reached a peak in 1993 when I was presented to the new President Clinton at a White House event. He asked where I was from and I told him Liverpool – not Canada or England. Despite living so far away from the Pier Head or The Cavern, I made sure that my camera batteries were regularly charged through visits, some of which were a little painful as I witnessed the city cope with new struggles. Still, Liverpool was my home and I had faith that resilience and strength of character would prevail. I was right.

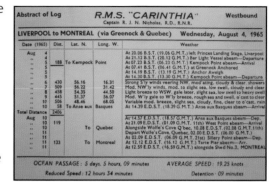

On one special visit to celebrate the role of Canada in the Battle of the Atlantic, I purchased Paul McMullin's book, *Liverpool The Great City*. I was moved almost to tears as he had captured the spirit of the city and through his superb work as an architectural photographer, its beauty and majesty. Paul showed that Liverpool is a beautiful city. Through the power of the internet I decided to contact him and thank him for what his work had done for me. That electronic link established us as friends. I have also been able to show so many friends the work of this wonderful photographer. Their response has always been one of amazement and new appreciation for my home. I am delighted to say that my visits back to Liverpool and to other great cities are now seen with a 'McMullin Eye.'

Tom Dykes, Burlington, Ontario, Canada
June 2015

INTRODUCTION
by Rob McLoughlin, OBE

The sound of breaking glass is the first thing I remember.

Not the song from Nick Lowe, released in the same year, but the crackling, sharp, icicle sound as glass was crunched beneath our feet. I recall looking down.

Today it would be trainers probably designer ones but from a discount store but then it was a strange black and red laced up American style sports shoe. Soft as a puppy.

We were trespassing, sure, but we were also investigating and capturing history.

Paul's shoes were harder, but only just. No steel toecap boots then! There were no helmets or yellow safety jackets either. I had a brightly coloured tank top which Elton John might have worn. It was, after all, Easter 1978. I was in awe; we were inside the abandoned Albert Dock in Liverpool.

'My Grandfather John worked here' I whispered to Paul who was busy taking pictures on a borrowed Mamiya C330 twin lens camera; 'My Father, Barney, must have unloaded ships here and my uncles'.

The light was magnificent. Shafts penetrated dark recesses of the empty warehouse through broken windows and the sky (light blue) was visible above and the building, falling about our ears, seemed haunted and full of memories of a bustling bygone age.
The stone stair wells and balconies towered above our unprotected heads for what seemed like miles and miles.

'Uncle Robert might have sailed from here?.'

I recalled the Uncle I'd never met who died aged 26 aboard HMS *Hampshire* which left the port and was mined by the Germans in controversial circumstances on 5th June 1916, just off the Orkneys. 255 crew and 7 passengers including Lord Kitchener died. 12 survived. My Dad said his brother had a premonition that if he sailed again for the King, he would die. Tragically it was true.
Then the moment. The picture which remains one of my favourites.

The Liver Birds peering above the dome of the Port of Liverpool building framed through the black, smashed and broken window of the dock building.

The shattered glass appears like clouds above the birds. It's breathtaking. In one shot Paul captured a metaphor for the decline, decay and conflict that was afflicting the city and which would worsen in the following decade.

In that decade, Paul would embark on his chosen career as a commercial and architectural photographer chronicling works for clients all over the world and then returning to his regular beat of simply knowing when to shoot the Liverpool

cityscape which is forever changing and developing. I started chronicling the decline of the port and primary industries first for Radio City and later for Granada Television and ITV. Thankfully also the revival – now accelerating.

I have called Paul 'Friend' since Infants School (St George's in Maghull) through Maricourt and onto Hugh Baird in Bootle where he really got the bug for photography. Then there we were, aged 18, scrambling over debris and walls to see the past and the future in one strange but daunting space.

Paul no longer has to trespass; he is thankfully invited in and as this magnificent book with Mike McNamee proves – that invitation benefits all of us.

He is an artist who just knows the moment. A privilege to call him 'friend' and to 'risk' my life with him on the Albert Dock; where I would return in the late 1980s to produce 'Granada Reports' from the Dock office.

I only wish I still had the 1978 sports shoes and the original vinyl copy of Nick Lowe's *Breaking Glass*.

Enjoy this superb book.

Rob McLoughlin, OBE
June 2015
www.robmcloughlin.com

Mid-summer sunrise.

THE WATERFRONT

This annotated panorama shows the principal buildings of the Liverpool Waterfront.

Alexandra Tower

City Lofts Apartments

Beetham Tower

West Tower

The Capital (formerly The Royal Insurance Building)

Malmaison Hotel

Unity Building

20 Chapel Street

The Atlantic Tower Hotel

St John's Beacon

The Church of Our Lady & St Nicholas Tower

The Roman Catholic Cathedral

The Cruise Liner Terminal

The Wellington Building

The Royal Liver Building

The Cunard Building

George's Dock Ventilation and Control Station

The Port of Liverpool Building

Pier Head Ferry Terminal

Mann Island Development

The Anglican Cathedral

Museum of Liverpool

The Albert Dock

The Wheel of Liverpool

Echo Arena and Convention Centre

Exhibition Centre Liverpool

CHAPTER 1

THE WATERFRONT

Liverpool's development has been dominated by its deep-water river frontage, the Waterfront. It was not always so and in earlier centuries the main port of the area was Parkgate on the River Dee. Liverpool slowly took the prominent position as the Dee silted up and ships became larger. To a local, the Waterfront is regarded as the area around the Three Graces – the Royal Liver Building, the Cunard Building and the Port of Liverpool Building. The skyline takes into view other buildings behind the docks and is bounded to the north by Alexandra Tower and to the south by the Anglican Cathedral. The Waterfront is somewhat disconnected from the city by the Strand, a busy eight-lane road. The name echoes its past as the original promenade, before the massive dock walls were built to harness the tides.

As a view, the Waterfront is best enjoyed from the famous Mersey Ferries, either from onboard or after you have landed at the Woodside or Wallasey Terminals. From there you can take in the whole expanse, centred on the Three Graces, but extending as far as the eye can see in either direction. The skyline has changed dramatically over the past two decades. Those of us who live on the Wirral side enjoy much the best view of the Waterfront with an uninterrupted view all the way from New Brighton down to Woodside.

The importance of the skyline is possibly greatest for the sailors who have made their way into the port over the centuries. The skyline tells them they are home, the familiarity of the outline defines their safe arrival. This has particular resonance for the dwindling number who sailed into the port, battered and bruised by the North Atlantic Convoys of World War II. How their brothers, lost at sea, would marvel at the famous skyline were they able to see it today.

> **"**…made from hammered copper plates, bolted together on an armature…**"**

One of the two famous Liver Birds which stand over 100 metres above the city, on top of the clock towers of the Royal Liver Building. One faces into the city while the other faces across the Mersey to the Wirral. Each bird is identical and they stand six metres high. The heads are just over a metre in length and the wings are three metres long. The mythical birds are made of hammered copper plates, bolted together on a structure of rolled steel joints. The designer was Carl Bernard Bartels (1866 – 1955) and the maker was George Cowper and the Bromsgrove Guild. During the xenophobia of the First World War, Bartels' contribution was erased from the records because he was of German origin; he was interred on the Isle of Man. The vapour trails are from over-passing flights en route to London or Europe which have passed over the Wallasey navigation beacon.

The Port of Liverpool building was the first of the
Three Graces to be built (1903 – 1907) and was the
headquarters of the Mersey Docks and Harbour Board.
The symmetrical building is a steel structure, encased in
concrete and faced with Portland Stone. The interior of
the central dome is a magnificent space, encircled with
the quotation, "They that go down to the sea in ships,
that do business in great waters. These see the works of
the LORD and his wonders in the deep".

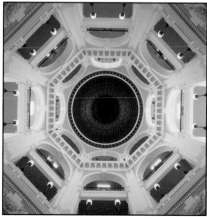

Initially 125 Superlambananas were commissioned to celebrate Liverpool Capital of Culture 2008. In 2010 a further eight were commissioned as a permanent piece of public art (known as the Eight for 08). Four of them are now located next to the Museum of Liverpool. All superlambanas were decorated in a unique fashion. The original, bright yellow, 17-foot sculpture now stands in Tithebarn St outside Liverpool John Moores University library building. The sculptor is a comment on both the danger of genetic engineering and the history of Liverpool in trading both sheep and bananas through its docks.

The Port of Liverpool Building reflected in the glass of the Mann Island Development.

“…Ferries have crossed the Mersey for centuries, starting around 1396…”

LEFT:
The new Pier Head Ferry Terminal. Opened in May 2009, it includes a café, restaurant, and visitor centre. Ferries have crossed the Mersey for centuries, starting around 1396.

THIS PAGE:
A view from the Albert Dock towards the Pier Head and Waterfront buildings.

ABOVE:
The Cunard Building was the last of the Three Graces to be completed in 1916. It was the headquarters of the Cunard Shipping Line and served as both offices and as a passenger terminal. Its design has now been attributed to Arthur J Davis, of Mewès and Davis.

RIGHT:
The Royal Liver Building of 1908–11 was designed to weather gracefully in the smoke of the time. It was restored to its original, pristine condition, almost a hundred years later. It was the second of the Three Graces to be constructed, basically of concrete reinforced with steel, with an exterior cladding of granite. The construction technique allowed the 10 main storeys to be built at an average rate of one floor every nineteen working days.

ABOVE:
The *Queen Elizabeth* visiting the city for Cunard's 175th anniversary. An estimated 1.3 million people came into the city to welcome her and her two sister ships.

RIGHT:
The return of large cruise-liners to Liverpool signals a resurgence of the city as a tourist destination. MV *Grand Princess* is moored at the ferry terminal adjacent to the Pier Head. The *Queen Mary 2* dwarfs the Isle of Man Steam Packet Company's high-speed catamaran, *HSC Manannan*. The view looks towards the north docks.

ABOVE:
Since 2011 the *Queen Mary 2* has been a regular visitor to the city. This view of the city looks to the south.

LEFT:
A super-telephoto lens was used from New Ferry on the Wirral, three miles distant.

Italian Renaissance detail on the frieze of the Cunard Building reflects the opulence of the first-class passenger lounge from which passengers embarked, whereas lower class passengers were accommodated in the basement, along with baggage handling and storage.

Canals return to the city. The Leeds-Liverpool Canal was intended to bring the goods of Lancashire industries to the port. This fell into decline with the emergence of the railways, but the waterway was recently re-opened and extended all the way to the Albert Dock. The re-opened Liverpool lock system brings narrow boats into Stanley Dock from where they can cruise onwards to the West Waterloo Dock, then Prince's Dock and across the front of the Three Graces, eventually arriving into the Albert Dock.

The flight of the locks at Wigan restricts the length of narrow boats compared with the standard for the rest of the UK. The 'Liverpool Short Boat' is 62 feet long but wider than normal at 14' 4" beam. Traditional Midlands craft cannot sail west of Wigan.

The George's Dock Ventilation Tower by Herbert Rowse. The two statues, in black basalt, by Edmund C THompson signify night and day to reflect the 24-hour operation of the Mersey Tunnel. Rowe's motorcyclist represents a modern Mercury, complete with racing helmet and goggles. One of the original toll booths from the 1934 Queensway Tunnel now stands at the foot of the building – these were replaced by automatic barriers.

❝ …Sir Peter is more widely known as the creator of the Beatles' sleeve for Sergeant Pepper's Lonely Hearts Club Band… **❞**

In 2015 Sir Peter Blake was commissioned by Liverpool Biennial, to design *Everybody Razzle Dazzle* which covers the Mersey Ferry *Snowdrop* with a distinctive pattern in monochrome and colour, transforming the vessel into a moving artwork as it continues its service. This is the third in the series of Dazzle Ship commissions and the first to be a working vessel. It is planned to keep this livery for two years.

Unlike other forms of camouflage, dazzle camouflage works not by concealing but by baffling the eye, making it difficult to estimate a target's range, speed and direction. Realised in monochrome and colour, each ship's dazzle pattern was unique in order to avoid making classes of ships instantly recognisable to enemy U-boats and aircraft.

Sir Peter is more widely known as the creator of the Beatles' sleeve for *Sergeant Pepper's Lonely Hearts Club Band.*

The Echo Arena and BT Convention Centre joined with the Exhibition Centre Liverpool (newly opened September 2015) and they occupy the site on the King's Dock adjacent to the Albert Dock and overlooked by the Anglican Cathedral. It was designed by two-times winner of the RIBA Stirling Prize for architecture, Wilkinson Eyre.

The Strand was originally a promenade directly on the seafront. The dock-building, and the height of walls needed to provide draught clearance for the ships moved the wharves and warehouses to the seaward side. Warehouses once occupied the middle of this busy thoroughfare (The Goree being the road on the right in this picture, with the Strand on its left).

The new Pier Head Ferry Terminal, opened in May 2009. On the top level is *Matou-Pan* Asian Restaurant.

On a cold winter's morning The Royal Liver Building is shrouded by mist. The public art, in Hope Street, reflects something of Liverpool's historical status as a centre for both immigration and emigration.

The Three Graces are relatively isolated when viewed from the air though very close to the Cruise Liner Terminal and the Albert Dock. The new canal section is linked through tunnels across from the Prince's Dock to the Albert Dock (on the right). The city extends backwards towards Aigburth and then onwards to Speke, John Lennon International Airport and the Manchester Ship Canal.

The now complete Mann Island Development showing neatly how the new buildings form a geodetic pattern but contrast sharply with the ornate Pier Head designs from early last century. However, they work in harmony with each other.

CHAPTER 2
THE ARCHITECTURAL HERITAGE

Although Liverpool suffered extensive bomb damage in 1941, the majority of significant buildings survived the devastation. Most of the buildings reflect the size and importance of the port, the majority of the land being taken over by docks, warehousing and commercial premises. By way of example, Liverpool University has only existed since 1903.

The drive for commercialism within and around the city means that only a single pre-eighteenth century building survives. The majority of the architecture is late Georgian, Victorian and Edwardian, built on a massive scale, which reflects the stature of the dock walls, designed to hold back the 30-foot tides. The first commercial, enclosed dock in the world was opened here in 1715.

The Blue Coat School (now The Bluecoat) was built in 1716 –18. Abolition of the slave trade in 1807 did not produce the expected demise of the port; more docks were built and the revenue increased many-fold. Between 1830 and 1930, nine million emigrants passed through Liverpool, some stayed and never travelled onwards!

The isolation of the port from its hinterland was relieved firstly by the spate of canal building, then with the completion of the world's first railway. Lime Street station was finished in 1836. St George's Hall soon followed on the land opposite, opening in 1854. In 1886 the Mersey Railway linked the Wirral with the port via the tunnel under the Mersey.

Without question it is the buildings around the Pier Head that are the most well known and provided a welcome sight for the convoys of Second World War shipping battling home through packs of U-boats. That was really the last act of major traffic to the actual Port of Liverpool and by the mid-'70s the south docks lay as a silent witness to the times that preceded it.

Initially Liverpool developed very rapidly as a commercial centre and many buildings were simply knocked down when they impeded progress. It is therefore ironic that the Albert Dock has risen from the dereliction and is now the UK's third busiest tourist attraction.

Development has been rekindled with the modification of the architectural heritage for other uses (mainly housing and leisure). Some of the newer buildings are exciting and adventurous in their design, especially those alongside the Three Graces providing a continuing link to the older, equally adventurous building of the late 1800s and early 1900s. Liverpool became the European Capital of Culture in 2008, a prestige that was accompanied by a spate of building, typified by Liverpool One. Liverpool - Maritime Mercantile City was inscribed as a cultural World Heritage Site by the UNESCO World Heritage Committee on 2 July 2004.

The Bluecoat.

Liverpool Town Hall is situated between Dale Street, Castle Street, Water Street and High Street, in the heart of the business district. Designed by John Wood, the building was opened in 1754, with various changes and revisions being made throughout the next 40 years. In 1795 the building was devastated by fire and was quickly rebuilt with the central dome completed in 1802 and the projecting portico (at the front, facing down Castle Street), completed in 1811.

The statue astride of the dome of the Town Hall is either Britannia or Minerva – modern thinking sides with Britannia but the records are inconclusive. She was erected in 1801–02.

Little remains of the original market and exchange other than the enclosed space of Exchange Flags. Much business was transacted in this open space and the nearby Corn Exchange. The memorial stands to Nelson's four victories at Cape St Vincent, the Nile, Copenhagen and Trafalgar. The statue was publicly funded in the aftermath of Nelson's death and almost £9,000 was raised in just over two months.

The former Royal Insurance building of 1896-1903, recently transformed into Aloft Liverpool hotel. It was built using a steel frame technique and is possibly one of the first in this country designed in this way.

LIVERPOOL The Great City

One of the many statues which are spaced around the gardens of St George's Hall. This one, *Save the Boy*, is a monument to Msg James Nugent who founded the Boy's Refuge. St George's Hall and Plateau, completed in 1839, is the second largest building in the city, giving way only to the Anglican Cathedral. It was built at a cost of £30,000 and includes a large public space (ball room), a small concert room, an assize (crown) court and a civil court. The design was the result of a competition won by Harvey Lonsdale Elmes and pioneered a heating and ventilation solution with a water fountain used to clean the air before it was re-introduced to the building. In 1969 the architectural historian Nikolaus Pevsner expressed his opinion that it is one of the finest neo-Grecian buildings in the world although the building is notable for its use of Roman sources as well as Greek ones. In 2004 the hall and its surrounding area were recognised as part of Liverpool's World Heritage Site.

The interior of St George's Hall.
The Minton floor tiles at St George's Concert Hall in Liverpool are normally covered by a protective flooring. The 30,000 hand-crafted Minton tiles, made in the English Potteries, are also used in the USA for the Capitol Building and the White House (as well as the Princes Road Synagogue) and were laid in 1852 to provide a hard surface for dancing. In 1954 when the tiles were uncovered for the first time since before the War, over 100,000 people queued to see the floor.

The Assize Court inside the St George's Hall. The original design competition was for both new courts and a public building. Harvey Lonsdale Elmes won both competitions and combined the designs into a single building. The court had a reputation for fast delivery of justice, often cases were of only six minutes duration and in effect there was a production line mentality.

Outside the front of the building, Queen Victoria rides
side-saddle and is wearing a ribband of the Order of St
George. The statue was ordered in bronze but following
concerns of the Liverpool Corporation's surveyor as
to its condition it was subsequently admitted by the
foundry that it was made of gun metal. It required
restorative work in 1885, just 15 years after installation.

The rear of St George's Hall. Many say that this should have been the front aspect of the building, with the beautiful St John's Gardens leading up to an entrance, however, this never materialised.

The small Concert Room was completed in 1856, two
years after the main hall.

The aerial view ahead of renovations to the Library shows the County Sessions House, Walker Art Gallery, Hornby Library and Picton Reading Room, and World Museum in the foreground. The circular end of St George's Hall holds the small concert room. Lime Street station can be seen behind the North Western Hotel.

Major General William Earle seems to point the visitors towards Wellington. Earle was killed while leading the rescue of Gordon, at Khartoum, taking an enemy bullet to the head. The statue was paid for by public subscriptions that were limited to two guineas (to encourage inclusiveness) and the monument was erected in December 1887. The Wellington Column was erected in 1863. It used to be possible to climb up to the top using internal stairs and the rails were secured for VE Day, in 1945, with scaffold poles. They remain there to this day as a memento of the occasion. A standard yard is sculpted into the base plaque.

The municipal buildings on Dale Street. Designed by John Wakeman and ER Robson, 1862–1868. The building brought together the scattered offices of Liverpool Corporation and remain in use to this day. The design is a mix of French Classic and Gothic Revival detail which has been praised and mocked in equal measure!

The Lime Street Gateway Concourse was completed in 2010. It was designed by Glenn Howells Architects.

Recently refurbished, Liverpool Lime Street station was an engineering feat of its day, the first fully-iron engine shed. The iron structure spans 200 feet and was constructed in 1879, the third station on the site in 40 years. When constructed in 1867 it had the largest span in the world but was almost immediately stripped of its title by St Pancras station in London. The second shed was added ten years later.

The most recent additions to the station concourse are statues of two Liverpool legends, Ken Dodd and Bessie Braddock. Bessie holds the 'Lion' branded egg, Doddy his trademark 'tickling stick'.

The Victoria Building of 1889–92 on Brownlow Hill was the main teaching and administrative building of the newly-formed university college. It was the inspiration of the term 'red-brick university' and is now the Victoria Gallery and Museum.

The interior of the VG&M. Here the Waterhouse café on the ground floor. The first and second floors house the art collections and museum.

ABOVE:
The cobbled carriageway leads past the recently-renamed Liverpool Museum, now World Museum, the Hornby Library and Picton Reading Room, Walker Art Gallery and the County Sessions House.

LEFT:
The Steble Fountain of 1879. It was always thought to have been cast in bronze but is actually cast-iron. It was named after Colonel RF Steble, mayor of the city in 1874.

Michelangelo (above) was sculpted by John Warrington
Wood in Rome in 1877. He sits at the entrance to
the Walker Art Gallery opposite another statue by
Warrington, this time of *Raphael*.

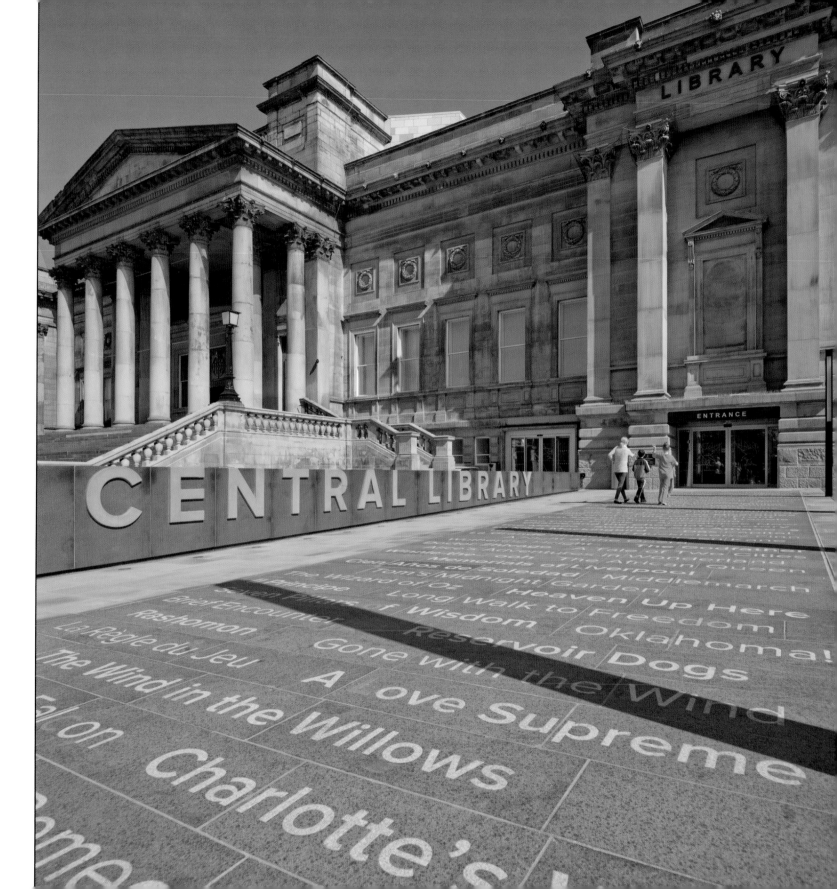

Liverpool Central Library was reopened to the public in May 2013 after extensive remodelling, at a cost of £50m, to provide 8,000 sq metres of library space across six floors. The architects Austin Smith Lord have designed a central atrium flooded with natural light from a domed glass roof. It connects to the Picton Library shown on the left and has won many architectural awards since completion.

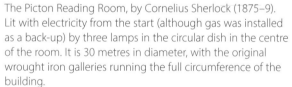

The Picton Reading Room, by Cornelius Sherlock (1875–9). Lit with electricity from the start (although gas was installed as a back-up) by three lamps in the circular dish in the centre of the room. It is 30 metres in diameter, with the original wrought iron galleries running the full circumference of the building.

Interior views of The Walker Art Gallery and the
splendid marble section.

LIVERPOOL The Great City

" …Martins Bank
by HJ Rowse
'probably the
best example
of 20th Century
American style
classicism' … "

LEFT:
The view down Water Street towards the Pier Head across the front of Martins Bank and the Town Hall.

RIGHT:
The interior of the former Martins Bank.

Every detail, right down to the stationery holders was overseen by the architect, Herbert Rowse.

FAR RIGHT:
The eighth-floor board room.

Peter Ellis designed Oriel Chambers (situated on Water Street) in 1864. It is the most significant office building in Liverpool and also one of the most important buildings in the world; it introduces the Modern Movement many years ahead of its time. The façade is an early example of cantilevered cladding design. The delightful, airy office space, is designed to illuminate the office workers' desks from three sides.

Peter Ellis also designed 16 Cook Street where he expanded on his use of glass for Oriel Chambers. It was completed in 1866 but was not well regarded and thought to be his last office design. Surprisingly open, with an exuberance of glass for a building erected in 1866, the interior contains a fine set of cast iron steps.

Parts of the city await restoration. This is the Pig and Whistle public house in
Chapel St. The port was famous for its pubs, some roads having almost one on every
corner. They formed meeting places for dockers as they waited the arrival of ships
and provided a place for gathering news of opportunities for work. Between pub
and church comes James Picton's Hargreaves Building (1859). The carved plaques
above the windows depict famous people who were involved in exploration of the
New World, an apt theme for one of the great staging ports for the Americas.

The Liverpool city guides will always tell visitors to make sure that they look up! Much of the heritage is detailed high on the building facades and goes un-noticed by the casual passer-by. Here we have (from top left): 3-5 Castle Street, Queen Insurance Building, Dale Street, the former Adelphi Bank on Castle Street (designed by WD Caröe circa 1891-2) and a salvaged panel from Colonial House.

Thirty James Street, formerly Albion House (White Star Line Building or Oceanic House) built in 1898 and designed by Richard Norman Shaw is very similar in design to New Scotland Yard in London. It was commissioned by J B Ismay the owner of the White Star Line whose office was situated in the bottom right-hand turret. It was from this building, that the list of survivors from the *Titanic* disaster were announced to crowds gathered on the Strand waiting for news . A poignant reminder of that fateful day in April1912.

The building has a Grade II* listed status and while the interior was modernised in the 1970s and 1980s with false ceilings and partitions, the exterior is remarkably unchanged except for an externally mounted clock and a simpler top gable end which was replaced after war damage. The building became 30 James Street after extensive interior refurbishment when it was transformed into a *Titanic* themed hotel (one of three in the city, the other being situated at the Stanley and Albert Docks).

Herbert Rowse designed the George's Dock Ventilation and Control Centre for the Mersey Road Tunnel which was opened by King V in July 1934. (See pages 28 and 29 for other features of this fine example of an Art Deco building.) It was reconstructed under the supervision of Rowse during 1951–2 following war damage. The red and white building (centre right) is another view of 30 James Street. The brick building in the centre is the George's Dock Pumping Station which is a listed building and houses two water pumps that drain the water from the underground railway tunnels. The Mersey Railway, opened from Liverpool James Street to Green Lane, Birkenhead running through the Mersey Railway Tunnel, one of the world's first underwater railway tunnels in 1886. The route was extended to Liverpool Central in 1890. A tunnelled branch to Birkenhead Park was added in 1888 to connect with the Wirral Railway and the original line extended to Rock Ferry to connect with the Birkenhead Woodside to Chester line in 1891.
The Mersey Railway was electrified in 1903 this being the world's first full electrification of a steam railway.

The India Building, the 1923 design by Herbert J Rouse. It was built for Alfred Holt & Co the shipping company. There is an underground access to James Street station below the building. It was completed in 1930 but extensively damaged by bombing in 1941 and then rebuilt by the same architect.

Canning Half Tide Dock is situated in the southern dock system, connected to Canning Dock to the east and Albert Dock to the south. The dock was designed by Jesse Hartley and opened in 1844. Hartley's revolutionary approach to moving and loading ships within the dock was rapidly made redundant by the arrival of steel-hulled vessels which, released from the constraints of grown timber, expanded and outgrew the space and, in particular, the entrances, all within two decades.

The 1913 steam tug *Kerne* is in the foregound. She is now the last remaining operational Naval coal-fired steamship to have seen service in two World Wars.

PREVIOUS PAGES
Gambia Terrace was once a choice dwelling place for sea captains and retains much of its splendour. The row was built in stages from the early 1830s to the 1870s and shows different styles of design from end to end. It has a commanding view of the Anglican Cathedral. The 1870 section is faced in yellow brick. Just seen behind the Terrace is the neo-classical church of St Bride with its six unfluted ionic columns. Built in 1829-30 it is the best surviving neo-classical church in the city.

The splendour of the buildings in the previous spread contasts sharply with those of these pages. Historically the Welsh towns provided Liverpool's warehousemen (there were 80,000 of them in the area) and they congregated in an area of housing that became known as the 'Welsh Streets'. The most famous of these 16 streets of terraced housing was Madryn Street, number nine being the birthplace of Beatle, Ringo Starr. In local parlance the area was 'tinned up' ahead of demolition but there remains some doubt about what is to happen to them. Coach loads of Beatles fans are often seen in the vicinity.

Liverpool has become a magnet
for film production companies and
some of the Welsh Streets have been
'distressed' ahead of period drama
filming.

LIVERPOOL The Great City

Great cities have the capacity to reinvent
buildings and their usage. The former 200 year-
old public house, The Whitehouse, on the corner
of Berry St and Duke St, was a Grade II listed
building. It was painted with a cat (or rat?) mural
in its derelict state by the artist, Banksy in 2004.
It became a 'must see' work of art. It is unclear
whether or not the mural was destroyed or
saved during the renovation of the building and
therefore its whereabouts are unknown.

Engraved markings in Roman numerals on the dock wall alongside the dock gate indicate the water level within the dock. Such matters were of concern to the dock workers as they tended the mooring ropes.

LIVERPOOL The Great City

The original Steers Dock of 1765 has been excavated and is open to the public for viewing. The viewing window situated adjacent to the John Lewis store gives little indication of what actually lies beneath the street.

The Victoria Tower, situated at the dock gates into the Mersey was built between 1847 and 1848 and designed by Jesse Hartley. It was described by Pevsner as 'All ham but tells of the commercial pride of the decades'. The tower's bell provided tidal and weather warnings to shipping.

The background to the view shows the northern docks towards Seaforth and now installed with wind turbines.

Great Howard Street runs parallel with the northern docks and heading back into the city. The ultra-modern Beetham Tower and West Tower contrast sharply with the rear of the Stanley Dock Tobacco Warehouse, architecturally just over 100 years apart, but in reality, a totally different world. This view is taken just north from the point where the Leeds-Liverpool Canal joins the Stanley Dock.

Canal narrow boats waiting to go through the Stanley Dock lock system on the Leeds–Liverpool Canal. The Stanley Dock tobacco warehouse can be seen beyond the railway bridge. This warehouse is said to be the largest brick built building in the world, a total of 27 million bricks being used in construction. Fireproof by design, it has been closed since 1980. Each floor is only 2.2m high, supposedly making it unsuitable for conversion to residential or office use. Built in 1901 it is a Grade II listed building. There have been numerous plans to redevelop the site and the building but these are yet to come to fruition. The Titanic Hotel has now opened on part of the site

LIVERPOOL The Great City

Much of the dock areas were designed with meticulous attention to detail. Granite was used to reinforce the corners of brick warehouse buildings where carts would pass, dockside edges were made with rounded granite inserts so that ropes would not snag as vessels were winched about. Even the waterside edges of the docks were slightly upturned to provide a tactile warning of the danger. The granite which lies at the heart of the build and design of Albert Dock was hewn from a quarry in Kirkcudbrightshire which was owned by the dock trustees. The random 'cyclopean' coursing of the blocks harks back to the Incas and was designed for maximum strength by the use of thin bedding and their survival for more than 150 years testifies to this skill. Almost 24m bricks and 47,000 tons of mortar were used in the building of the Albert Dock. In a further example of close detailing the names of the docks were labelled in chiselled granite.

The tradition of granite work has been continued to this day. On the left, the public area around the new canal extension, in front of the Three Graces, is detailed in massive granite blocks.

LEFT:
The drinking fountain is one of a number which were installed in the mid 19th century, commonly called a 'Melly' fountain, after the philanthropist Charles P Melly. Though most of his fountains were made from red, Aberdeen granite, this example is cast iron. It is situated on Regent Road at Nelson Dock. It is one of 33 sanctioned in 1859 by the Mersey Docks and Harbour Board in a futile attempt to keep the dockers out of the local public houses!

CHAPTER 3

THE CATHEDRALS AND CHURCHES

For a city with such a wealthy history Liverpool has very few churches. Much of the architecture was dominated by the commercial need to warehouse the vast quantities of goods being delivered into the port. The crowning glories of the city's ecclesiastical architecture are its two cathedrals. Although they are joined by the same street, in an architectural sense they are as far apart as they could be. The Anglican cathedral, dedicated to St James, was started in 1904 with the city at its peak of prosperity and was finished in 1978 when the long decline was at its lowest point. The building is massive in scale, the largest Anglican cathedral in Christendom. It shares the other end of Hope Street with the Roman Catholic Metropolitan Cathedral, itself a building of remarkable design with a centre altar and a congregation of 2,000 seated in a sweeping arc around it.

The other churches are somewhat dwarfed by the scale of the cathedrals but there are some architectural gems dotted about the city. The Greek Orthodox church of St Nicholas is outstanding and just visible above the Waterfront skyline. Its decorative brickwork is an echo of Shaw's Albion House, itself modelled on his own New Scotland Yard building. It is actually a close copy of the St Theodore church in Constantinople. Also noteworthy is the Swedish Seaman's church (1884), a riot of brickwork windows, arches and spires. The Princes Road synagogue is also a religious building of considerable importance.

The denominations of the churches reflects the mix of people who moved into the city to find work. Although many think of Liverpool as a suburb of Ireland, there were an almost equal number of Welsh labourers and their families. This is reflected in the churches; by 1891 the census shows 26 Roman Catholic and 27 'Welsh' churches. A generalised demarcation is that Irish labour manned the docksides and Welsh labour the warehouses. Wales also provided quite a number of skilled building trades' people and the regular packet steamers to Llandudno provided a link with their homes and families.

The Metropolitan Cathedral of Christ the King.

ABOVE:
The original plan for the Metropolitan Cathedral was a much grander affair and was scaled back on cost grounds after completion of the crypt. An echo of the design remains as the 'Dome of Home' high above the town of New Brighton at the mouth of the Mersey. This is the first thing that incoming sailors catch sight of as they enter the port.

The Lutyen's Crypt, the only surviving part of Edwin Lutyen's grand design for the second largest cathedral in the world. War and rising costs saw the original plan scrapped and all that remains of the idea is a model in the Museum of Liverpool at Mann Island (see previous page).

Lutyen's bold move for grandeur was replaced by the adventurous design of Sir Frederick Gibberd. Work began in 1962 and the building was consecrated in 1967. Today it is flanked on the far side by the new Liverpool University Arts Building designed by Rick Mather and by the two Liverpool Science Park buildings.

The Anglican Cathedral was started in time to lay the foundation stone in 1904 and completed 74 years later on 25 October 1978. It is a huge building, the Lady Chapel at the lower right is larger than most parish churches and is an architectural jewel in its own right. It has the largest and heaviest peal of bells in the world. The tower rises to more than 330 feet. The building is 619 feet in length. Examining the old photographs of the construction shows relatively few workmen, never more than ten in any one picture. Despite this they laid a little short of five million bricks!

LIVERPOOL The Great City

LIVERPOOL FEMALE ORPHAN ASYLUM.

Ann Davis,	Aged 11 years, Died 26.May 1844.
Alice Buckley,	Aged 9 years, Died 9. April 1845.
Ann Ellis,	Aged 10 years, Died 16. June 1846.
Eliz^th Williams,	Aged 13 years, Died 2. May 1847.
Sarah B. Moss,	Aged 10 years, Died 18.May 1847.
Marg^t Hegan,	Aged 8 years, Died 30.May 1847.
Charlotte Boyd,	Aged 11 years, Died 18.April 1849.
Ann Sumner,	Aged 9 years, Died 30.Novr 1849.
Eliz^th Hughes,	Aged 11 years, Died 22.June 1850.
Jane E. Garner,	Aged 14 years, Died 28.Augt 1850.

The gravestones of the adjacent St James' Cemetery are a lasting memorial to the many who died in the crowded, unsanitary conditions of the mid-nineteenth century. This example is to the orphaned girls who died – none reached the age of 15 years. Liverpool pioneered a number of intitiatives to assist the poor and improve their daily lives. Wash-houses, The Bluecoat School, workshops for the blind, institutes for the deaf and dumb, the public health movement and many others originated in the city.

"...A cathedral fit for a city of
the stature of Liverpool..."

Bishop Chavasse

LEFT:
From the air the immense scale of the cathedral is more apparent. Gambier Terrace flanks the right-hand side in the picture. The housing, offices and university complex, to the left of the cathedral in the picture, have been sympathetically designed. The St James' gardens surround the cathedral on three sides. There is a sloping promenade down to the gardens which contain many grave stones and the Huskisson Memorial. He was a local MP and the first fatal casualty of the railway era, being knocked down on the opening day of the Liverpool–Manchester railway and later dying of his injuries.

TOP RIGHT:
The memorial stone to Kitty Wilkinson, the founder of the first public Wash House in 1842 after outbreaks of cholera in 1832 and 1840.

MIDDLE:
The Oratory, situated adjacent to the cathedral. This is the former mortuary chapel to St James' Cemetery and was designed by John Foster Jr in the style of a Greek Doric temple. Built 1829.

BOTTOM RIGHT:
The Ramps. Another design by John Foster Jr, intended to allow funeral processions to descend into the cemetery and for the mourners to promenade. The Huskisson Memorial can be seen right. John Foster Jr was a prominent Liverpool corporation surveyor b1786 d1846. He is also buried here.

Regardless of whether it is viewed from a distance or up close the Anglican
Cathedral is an imposing sight.

The interior of the cathedral is relatively plain and uncluttered, giving a great sense of space. The chair arrangement may be varied to suit the church-service requirements and a huge open lift can take them down to an underground store.

The church of Our Lady and St Nicholas tower. Built 1811–1815. The nave was rebuilt in 1952 because of war damage. In 1810 the original (1774) church also suffered a bizarre accident when the tower collapsed under the weight of the pealing bells and fell onto the Sunday congregation below. Twenty-three girls from the Moorefield's Charity School died in the incident.

LIVERPOOL The Great City

LEFT:
Liverpool has played host to many nationalities, ethnicities and religions. The Chinese Archway was constructed by Chinese craftspeople in 2000. The local China Town is one of the oldest in the country, more than a century in the city. The arch stands alongside the Great George Street Congregational church (1840–1), locally known as the 'Blackie'. Recently refurbished it is still known as the 'Black E' and is a centre for the arts and the community.

THIS PAGE:
Always known as the 'bombed out church'. The church of St Luke stands at the top of Bold Street and Berry Street. Built by the corporation under the auspicies of John Foster Sr, around about 1805. It was eventually completed by John Foster Jr in 1827 who succeeded his father as corporation surveyor. The church serves as a war memorial.

St Andrew's Presbyterian church 1823 on Rodney Street. This was designed by John Foster Jnr who was also responsible for Gambia Terrace and the Ramps of the Anglican Cathedral. St Andrew's has recently undergone refurbishment as student accommodation.

"…it provided a wholesome but attractive alternative to pub and music hall…**"**

Central Hall on Renshaw Street was opened in 1905; its main auditorium seated almost 2,500 people. It provided a wholesome but attractive alternative to pub and music hall with concerts and other social activities. It is a most unchurch-like building. In the background is the Adelphi Hotel.

"…He who has not
seen the interior of
Princes Road synagogue
in Liverpool has not
beheld the glory of
Israel….**"**
         H.A. Meek (1993)

The Princes Road synagogue has been described as one of the finest examples of Orientalism in British synagogue architecture. The view that greets the visitor as they enter the central doors is quite astounding. The ornate Bitmah (reading platform) leads on towards the pulpit, behind which stands an Ark, decorated in polished red granite and crowned with five, deep blue domes, which are in turn, decorated with gold stars. The lower levels reflect a heavy 'Moorish' influence in the design while the rose windows at either end are typically European in design, if not in their geometric detail. This Grade 1 listed building was the design of the brothers, W and G Audsley and it opened in 1874 as the finest example of their work. The building costs were substantially contributed by David Lewis (of the Lewis' Department Store) but the community has contributed much to the local arts, political and business life. As a staging post towards America, a great many Russo-Polish Jews came to Liverpool and got no further – their descendants still form part of the present congregations.

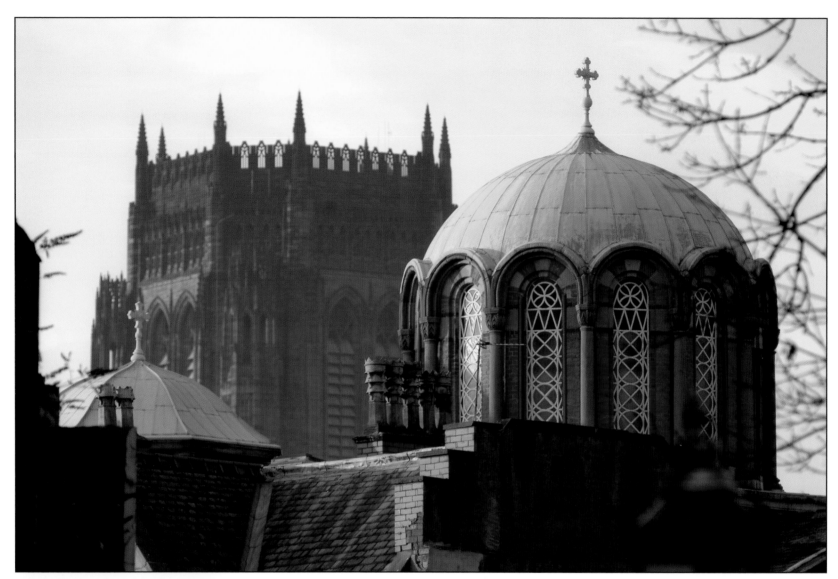

ABOVE:
The Greek Orthodox church, which was built in 1870, is situated just a few yards along Princes Road from the synagogue. The 'Welsh Presbyterian Cathedral' is situated a little further up the road as is the Roman Catholic church of St Margaret to complete this cluster of religious buildings.

LEFT:
The *Gustav Adolfs Kyrka* known locally as the 'Swedish Seaman's church'. Built in 1883–4.

RIGHT:
The former St Peter's Catholic church on the south side of Seel Street. The church was opened on 7 September 1788. It served as a Catholic church for 188 years. In 1976, it was transferred to the Polish community and it is still referred to as 'the Polish church'. It held its last service in 1978. It is now *Alma de Cuba*, a very upmarket restaurant and bar. It was the first church building in Liverpool to be turned into a social venue.

CHAPTER 4

LEISURE AND TOURISM

There are many facets to the status of Liverpool as a tourism and leisure city. The Albert Dock is a World Heritage Centre and a major attraction but, in the main, people do not come to the city just to admire Jesse Hartley's 'pile of bricks'. It is, however, of such importance that it has its own chapter at the end of this book.

To the outsider, the city is most closely associated with music and football, it is rare that a local has to explain in detail where they are from when visiting any other part of the world. Historically, Liverpool has received an eclectic mix of cultures and races because of its prominent position as a seaport and staging post to the far reaches of the old empire. The tourist mix therefore comprises those who are returning to their roots and those who are curious to see just where Lennon, McCartney, Starr and Harrison hung out. One of the most frequent comments the natives of the city hear is that their guests cannot believe what a handsome city Liverpool is. The Waterfront, viewed from either the other side of the Mersey, or from the famous Mersey Ferry, is a spectacular sight and one of the aims of this book has been to illustrate just how much it has changed since the Millennium.

Good tourist destinations need a mixture of attractions, including shops. Liverpool has two impressive cathedrals, a wonderful collection of public buildings, a waterfront, museums, galleries but, until recently had lagged a little on the shopping front. The concept for Liverpool One was to provide a new shopping district which linked the major attractions of the Waterfront to the city centre, nightlife and cathedrals. This was accomplished by appointing a single overseeing developer (from 47 applicants) who then proceeded to engage the services of a large number of architectural practices, who were effectively cut loose to be as creative as possible. The only stipulation was that a covered mall was not permissible. Liverpool One has achieved almost all of its aims. The Albert Dock is now just a stone's throw from the start of the shopping area of Liverpool One and this provides a natural conduit into the rest of the city.

Any large city is something like an onion. At the core are the major attractions, the Beatles Experience, the Mersey Ferry, the Three Graces, the cathedrals. Outside of this there are the gems that only the enthusiastic traveller gets to – the galleries, the UK's second largest collection of public statues, the churches of other denominations, China Town, the list could go on and on.

RIGHT:
A centre piece of the museum's exhibits is a section from the Liverpool Overhead Railway along with an original carriage. It was opened in 1893 as the world's first electric elevated railway and was known locally as the 'Docker's Umbrella'. It was dismantled in 1957. The steam locomotive alongside is the 1838 *Lion* which ran on the Liverpool to Manchester Railway. She appeared in three films, *Victoria the Great* (1937), *The Lady and the Lamp* (1951) and *The Titfield Thunderbolt* (1952). She had finished her life as a stationary pumping engine at Princes Dock before being rescued by The Liverpool Engineering Society.

ABOVE:
The Liverpool One development, Paradise Street. Part of the design aspect was that iconic buildings could be viewed at various points.

RIGHT:
The Wheel of Liverpool. The 60 metre high tourist attraction is positioned on the piazza outside the Liverpool Echo Arena and Convention Centre – near to the Albert Dock.

The wheel includes 42 fully enclosed, air-conditioned capsules offering riders spectacular panoramic views of the city, the River Mersey, the Welsh mountains and the World Heritage Site waterfront.

ABOVE:
The Liverpool Sailors' Home gateway originally stood on the site of the current John Lewis building just to the left of this picture. It is now located at the end of Paradise Street.

RIGHT:
Design for the 42-acre Liverpool One development was deliberately commissioned with a number of architectural practices so that there would be a range of styles and approaches. This view looks down Paradise Street from the John Lewis store. Liverpool One is the largest open-air shopping centre in the UK.

LIVERPOOL The Great City

Liverpool One. Built at a cost of £750m, Grosvenor Developments were behind the scheme to transform the heart of Liverpool. Employing 27 different firms of architects with master-planning by BDP.

Chavasse Park. Part of the Liverpool One project, this park with its wide expanse of grass and sloping walkways has fast become a place of relaxation and a meeting place. The Reverend Francis James Chavasse was appointed Bishop of Liverpool in 1900 and masterminded the plans to build Liverpool Cathedral. His son, Noel served with distinction in World War I, being the only soldier to win two Victoria Crosses.

RIGHT:
Peters Lane Arcade, again part of the Liverpool One project. Designed by Dixon Jones Architects, this arcade uses a clever design of roof to give natural, even illumination, even on dull days.

The Liverpool One Bridewell on Campbell St
(Campbell Sq) of 1861 was once the lock-up and
offices for the local police force. Today you may
dine discretely at tables set in the old cells.

ABOVE:
The John Lennon Suite of the Hard Day's Night Hotel and the statue of John Lennon in Mathew Street. The hotel has commanding views of the city.

RIGHT:
The hotel was opened in 2008 and is a Beatles-themed, luxury hotel. The building was formerly called Central Buildings and was designated as the backup location for the Allied Command Headquarters in the city, during the Battle of the Atlantic. Later it was used as offices on the upper floors and also housed the famous De Coubertins sports bar immediately prior to its closure and conversion. The building dates back to 1884 and was designed by Thomas C Clarke.

Across the road from the Philharmonic Hall is the Philharmonic Hotel, of 1898–1900. The brewer, Robert Cain, felt that the drinking public should be exposed to the enlightenment of quality architecture and the interior is ornately decorated in marble, mahogany and glass. This even extends to the famous gentlemen's toilet and users of the facility have always to be prepared for the invasion of camera-toting tourist parties!

In July 2011 Everyman Theatre was closed for complete rebuilding . Originally the 1837 building was constructed as Hope Hall, a dissenters' chapel. In 1841 it became a church dedicated to Saint John the Evangelist. This became a public concert hall in 1853. In 1912 the hall was turned into Hope Hall Cinema, which continued serving this purpose until it closed in 1963. During the 1970s and the 1980s works of Liverpool playwrights, including Willy Russell and Alan Bleasdale, received debuts in the theatre: these included *Shirley Valentine* and *John, Paul, George, Ringo … and Bert*.

In October 2014, the Stirling Prize was awarded to
Haworth Tompkins by the Royal Institute of British
Architects for the best British building of the year.
The front of the building displays 105 punched
aluminium panels featuring life-sized images of
Liverpool residents.

The interior of the rebuilt Everyman Theatre.

LIVERPOOL The Great City

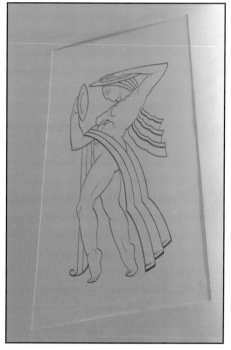

The Philharmonic Hall. The home of the Liverpool Philharmonic Orchestra, this building was designed by Herbert J Rowse after the original building was destroyed by fire in 1933 and rebuilt soon after. Depending upon your point of view, the plain-styled, brick-built exterior, is ugly or sophisticated. The interior, however, has a wonderful accoustic space and the image here shows the daunting view a nervous soloist would face as they came up on stage. Incised Art Deco female figures, representing musical moods, adorn the walls of the auditorium.

The Giant Marionettes, designed and operated the
French street theatre company, Royal de Luxe have
made two visits to the city to date. The first in 2012
commemorated the 100th anniversary of the sinking
of the *Titanic*, the second the 100th anniversary of
World War I. Both attracted huge crowds as the massive
puppets paraded across the city.

ABOVE: *Peace and Harmony*, the monument dedicated to the memory of John Lennon by American artist, Lauren Voiers.

RIGHT:
The statue of Eleanor Rigby sits in Stanley Street and depicts the subject of the famous Beatles' tune of 1966. *Eleanor Rigby* was actually the b-side of the single *The Yellow Submarine*. The sculptor was the singer, Tommy Steele, who donated the piece to the people of Liverpool in 1982 at a cost of three pence – an allusion to his show *Half a Sixpence*. Since its release 40 years ago, the tragic heroine of this two-minute Lennon McCartney masterpiece has become a source of endless fascination for Beatles' enthusiasts.

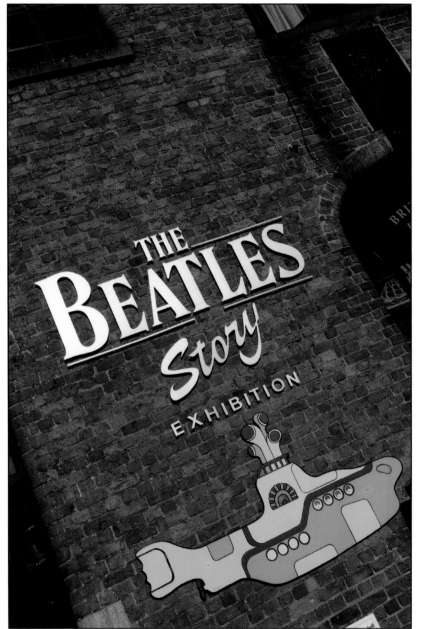

ABOVE:
The Wheel of Liverpool is now positioned on the piazza of the Echo Arena. At 60 metres high it provides stunning views of the city from each of its 42 capsules.
LEFT:
The influence of the Beatles is evident across many parts of the city. Here the Yellow Submarine announces the presence of the Beatles Story Exhibition at the Albert Dock.

Western Approaches Museum.
The Western Approaches Command HQ was responsible for control of the Western Approaches during WW II, the main sea route from the Americas to Great Britain. It was relocated from Plymouth to Liverpool in 1941. Situated in the basement of Derby House, part of Exchange Buildings, it was known locally as the *citadel* or *fortress* due to the extensive reinforced concrete protection.
The museum is open from 1st March to October each year.

CHAPTER 5

THE ALBERT DOCK

The climax of dock building for the Port of Liverpool came in 1846 when Prince Albert opened the new complex named after him and after the expenditure of £721,756. The dock and the surrounding buildings addressed the need to provide a secure berth in a river with a large tidal range, as well as compliance with the 1803 Warehousing Act. This act permitted importers of taxed goods to defer payment of the excise duties (provided the goods were securely stored and supervised) until they were moved to their place of sale – as today, it was all about cash flow. This security requirement influenced the architectural design of the docks complex with its high walls, policemen's lodges and controlled gates. Goods travelled only a matter of yards from the ship's hold to their warehouse floor. In addition, the value of the cargo placed a requirement for a fireproof environment so as to reduce the costs of insurance. Devastating fires at both Liverpool and Hamburg in 1842 had highlighted the fire problem once again, and a number of full scale mock-ups of the Albert Dock buildings were tested to destruction before the architect Jesse Hartley was happy with his designs. It was the close proximity of the warehouse elevations to the water's edge which later prevented any modifications to the complex and this accelerated the eventual demise of the Albert Dock.

The arrival of ever-larger iron ships, no longer constrained by the strength and length of timber meant that the Albert Dock soon became too small and by 1914 hardly any ships actually unloaded there, although the warehouses continued in profit until the 1950s, storing tobacco, wines and spirits. After a number of false starts and some threats of demolition, the complex was eventually saved, restoration starting in earnest in 1983. The refurbished buildings now hold museums (including the Beatles Story), an art gallery (Tate Liverpool), dwelling apartments, commercial offices and shops. The complex is the UK's most popular heritage attraction and has most recently been linked up with the new Liverpool One development which is just the other side of the Dock Road and provides a conduit into the city centre. The area sometimes reverts to its past, as a bustling seaport, when period dramas are filmed and the walkways are filled with costume-clad extras and sailing schooners are once again moored dockside.

The Albert Dock complex is laid out in five separate warehouse stacks, each five storeys high, but none having the same floor plan. They are: The Colonnades (where Tate Liverpool is situated); Edward Pavilion; Atlantic Pavilion; Britannia Pavilion and Warehouse D (which houses the Maritime Museum).

The 1843 swing bridge spanning the passage between the Canning Half Tide Dock and Albert Dock. It is the last surviving example of a design from John Rennie's London Dock and was supplied by the Haigh Foundry, Wigan. The railings to the north pivot flat to prevent fouling with ship's ropes when swung open.

This vantage point is one of the best for viewing the whole of the Albert Dock area.

An overview of the northern part of the Albert Dock includes the Pump House on the right and the Edward Pavilion to the left. They flank the 1848 Dock Traffic Office , designed by Phillip Hardwick, with its cast iron Tuscan portico. Hartley added a second floor flat to house the principal clerk, along with the splendid tapering chimney stacks just a year later.

The 1855 rebuilt gable end of the Salthouse Dock Transit Shed. This provides tourists with an iconic framing for the Three Graces and the Mann Island development. The name Salthouse Dock reflects the once considerable importance of the salt industry in the seventeenth and eighteenth centuries. Coal from Lancashire was brought to Liverpool to refine rock salt from Cheshire, and manufactured salt was brought down from Northwich. There was an extensive business community buying, selling and exporting salt to such places as the Isle of Man and (later) Newfoundland for salting fish. After Albert Dock opened, Salthouse Dock was used mainly for loading vessels, which had discharged in Albert. Much of the masonry now visible dates from improvements made in 1842 and 1855, but some of that at the south west corner is original.

The exquisite detailing of the granite work can easily be overlooked as the viewer concentrates on the buildings in the distance.

The view of the Albert Dock complex from One Park West shows the Canning Dock (bottom right) the Half Tide Dock (right centre) and the Salthouse Dock (left). The Graving Dry Dock is just visible on the middle right. The wet docks are interconnected by passages and these were to lead to the decline of the docks after the 1860s – they were simply too narrow for the larger screw-propelled steamships. World War II provided a brief reprieve for the dock when it was used as a base for escort vessels in the Battle of the Atlantic.

The lower view is across the Canning Dock of the Mann Island development.

Acknowledgements

With grateful thanks to all companies and individuals who have helped with the making of this book and who gave access to interesting vantage points. Clients have commissioned some images and we thank them for allowing their use within the book.

We have drawn extensively upon the great scholarship of Joseph Sharples, John Belchem, and Quentin Hughes to guide us around the city and its history, we thank them all.

National Museums Liverpool, Matou-Pan Asian Restaurant, Liverpool One Bridewell, Alaster Burman, Kevin Evans – One Park West, Neil McKenzie of Epson UK, Kevin Stott – Liverpool Cathedral, Liverpool One, RIBA NW, ISG Construction, Grosvenor Estates, Liverpool Civic Trust, Liverpool Hard Days Night Hotel, Castlewood Property Management, Cunard Buildings, Holiday Inn Hotel, 30 James Street Hotel, The Victoria Gallery and Museum, Mersey Travel, The Western Approaches, Dominic Beaumont – The Everyman Theatre, Denis, Curtins Consulting Engineers, Liverpool Chamber of Commerce, Rob McLoughlin, Tom Dykes.

The Last Word

It is now 11 years since our first book in the series, *A Portrait of Liverpool*, was published. The cranes in the foreground above are likely to be some of the last to irritate photographers! The remaining large-scale project is the new Royal Liverpool Hospital which has an estimated completion date of 2017. Sadly there seem to be no new plans for constructing iconic buildings in the city, although the Liverpool Waters Development of the Northern Docks may once again bring a Stirling Prize-winning building to the area. The Everyman Theatre is a great example of a modern, iconic building, designed to harmonise with its surroundings, well worthy of its many awards. The three Queens, berthed in the River Mersey (named Victoria, Mary then Elizabeth) to celebrate Cunard's 175th year in the city, provide a continuity from the days of sail to Liverpool the Great City.